THE ROAD

"In whose heart are the highways to Zion."
Ps. 84. 5.

By the same Author
THE STARTING PLACE OF PRAYER

First published
November, 1935
Printed and bound in Great Britain
at the works of
W. HEFFER & SONS, LTD.
Cambridge, England.

Republished
December, 2015
SILENT LINES
Edinburgh, UK
www.silentlines.co.uk

Cover art
RUTH ACHESON
www.ruthacheson.com

Foreword.

> *"The seeds that fell on the good soil represent honest, good-hearted people who hear God's word, cling to it, and patiently produce a huge harvest.*
> (Luke 8:15, New Living Translation)

Naomi Claire Sherwood was someone I knew very little about until I found this book while working through the belongings my grandparents had left us in their house in Charing, Kent, UK. Naomi Claire, Claire to her family, was my great grandmother. The Road is a collection of church services - prayers, poetry, liturgy, meditations - which she wrote over a period of time in the early 20th century. Following the encouragement of friends, who saw in these services something that should be shared beyond her immediate church circle, she published this collection in 1935. Eighty years later, I have undertaken to republish The Road, seeing in it something that should be shared beyond her generation.

Each service is a journey saturated with the truths of scripture, masterly crafted together to encourage both praise and reflection. Sentences which continue to haunt me ("Shall it be said of us and of our generation..."), and sentences which are like a breath of fresh air ("May the beauty of thy holiness flood our souls...") have heightened to me the intemporal wonder of the truths we hold dear, bringing new depth to my own prayer life as I borrow from hers.

Her writings suggest a resilient and powerful joy, cultivated by clinging fast through many trials. She was no stranger to sorrow. A strict upbringing with little praise, the spiritual and familial estrangement of her brother the poet James Elroy Flecker, his jealousy of Claire's "normal" life approved of by their parents, his early death, a period of what was probably post natal depression before the days of a recognised diagnosis, a strained relationship with my grandfather who was seen to have brought along this period of darkness, my grandfather's fondness for his late Uncle and his widow, in whom he saw kindred wounded soul rejected by his own family, and her own ill health which brought her life to an early end. Her prayers pull no punches, allowing us to see something of the strength of her convictions and the authenticity of her faith. Through the reality of our temporary broken dwelling, she points us to our eternal unblemished home.

These services also display a generosity of spirit and a desire to celebrate the common ground in a diverse Christian tradition. Possibly as a reaction against her parents' strict orthodoxy, but more likely out of sheer delight in the One these different traditions celebrate in their own way, her heart is set on her Saviour and Him alone, the head of the Church, who cleanses and unites us all by his death and resurrection.

In republishing this collection of services, I have remained faithful to the original content (bar my all-time favourite typo: "thy dumble servants"). The original acknowledgements included page numbers, which I have replaced with chapter titles, for transferability between a hard copy and an electronic copy. In addition to the original content, I have provided the lyrics from each of the hymns mentioned in the services as an appendix.

My prayer in this endeavour is that through a legacy Claire could not have foreseen ("what do you mean, an electronic book?"), we readers can both witness and be inspired by a life which cries out the following: hear the truth, cling to it, and patiently produce a huge harvest.

CARA THOMPSON.

Preface.

To find God is our satisfaction and our joy. We can help one another in the discovery of Him. All of us are on the same quest, hindered by the same difficulties, sharing the same hunger and thirst after God, resting in the same assurance that we do find Him ever more and more fully. We help one another most when we pray together.

There are two uses of corporate prayer. The one springs from our sense of membership in the community and is concerned with the general needs and worship of the community as a whole. The other leads through, and by means of, the corporate to the personal, and is the function of the services in this book. That is why I have called it "The Road". None of these services is a completed act of worship until the individual spirit has entered into its own communion with God.

All over the country there are groups of people seeking to know God through this way of corporate prayer, and to each one of us this communion is a necessity. We may be at the beginning of the day, full of its plans and possibilities, or at the end, tired and self-concerned over our individual successes and failure. Before we can either move out rightly to envisage the day, or take our true rest, we must tread the path of worship. Strength for worship, detachment from our immediate surroundings, can be gained by a corporate act which, making us one of a company, lifts us out of ourselves and sets our whole being on the pilgrim way towards God. These services may help to set our feet on the road.

Or, to take a modern metaphor from flying. At first

we are on the ground, surrounded by all the bustle of departure, last words from friends, chatter about the machine. Then the propeller is swung, and the plane moves forward, on wheels, along the ground. But we don't stay there. That very movement that started us has also lifted us. The ground recedes and we mount steadily upwards. These services are intended to fulfil the function of starting.

In an appendix I have set out the lines along which services such as these can be drawn up, because this collection is meant to be suggestive of the host of ideas which can be used, the endless variety of material available, the matchless wealth of our English tongue in devotional speech. With regards to those printed here, each service should be looked on as a drama of religious experience. Everything depends on the approach made to it. If it is merely read through by someone "taking prayers" to a group of listeners there can be no hope of success. Each service needs careful preparation by the reader, and a realisation of the sequences. May I say that nothing has been put in either for the sake of length or of including a certain item. Each piece, whether text, poem, hymn, prayer or versicle and response is meant in my mind to fulfil a definite part in that drama of which man's soul is the stage and in which the hosts of heaven enact a spiritual chorus.

The services are meant to move through definite progressions, such as are found in the office for Holy Communion, which ascends peak by peak, perhaps lowering the level in between for a moment, preparatory to a further climb, a method of ascent that all good mountaineers know. The same method is also found in that much-maligned service of mattins. It may be the urbanisation of our life that has caused it so to fall into disrepute. In the country, especially on a sunny Sunday morning, the sense of comparative cessation from toil, the donning of better clothes and clean, which is no mean feat where water has to be fetched cold from the well instead of springing hot from the tap, the gathering together in the place where for generations each family has prayed, rejoiced and sorrowed, all contribute to give a reality and grandeur which no one will lightly disregard. It is an intelligible, a "reasonable" worship, and rises steadily to heights of splendid praise.

This is not a digression to air my opinions. I am sure that one of the most powerful aids to individual spiritual growth is the regular participation in a worship that is concerned with God and His children rather than with ourselves. It is one of the most healthy signs of the times that we are at last learning the lesson that our worship if it is to be true must be centered on God, His nature, His activity, His grace, manifested in a myriad ways in the world, supremely in Jesus Christ, the altogether lovely. It is as we train our minds and thoughts to dwell on God that we prepare ourselves to receive the vision of Himself which is ever awaiting, in ever fuller measure those who have eyes to see. God does rule in the affairs of men, and the effort to enter into an understanding of His will and purpose for the world, both by prayer and conduct, will achieve the harmony we long for.

One of the biggest difficulties in worship, especially when it occupies so short a space of time as these services, arises out of wandering thoughts. We are often warned against them and advised to drive them sternly away. I would rather suggest that at the outset of worship, in the silence that precedes it, they should be given a definite, *ungrudging* place; that whatever is at the moment of going to worship the dominant interest of our conscious mind should be accepted, and that we should, as the first step towards worship, seek out the connection between that activity or thought and God. For God is concerned with our life; there is nothing we cannot link with Him by whom the very hairs of our head are numbered. For example: is the thought uppermost in my mind the joyful anticipation of meeting a friend? I can readily bring that to Him in whom all friendships are enriched, and go on my way knowing that our meeting will be enhanced by His participating Presence. Is it pleasurable satisfaction in some success, in some game well played? God is the Lord of all good life, and rejoices in the activity and well-being of His creatures. Or is it the sense of failure, burden, monotony, discouragement, shame? He is the lifter-up of our head; He can put a well of music in our soul; He offers us to share His yoke and plough through the day beside Him. In this way out of what might have been hindrances we build our daily altars of praise.

My grateful thanks are due to several authors and publishers whose names are noted in the Acknowledgements, for material which they have generously allowed me to use; to Miss V. A. Tritton, for her many suggestions, by which this book could be made more widely useful; to Mr. J. H. Procter, for valuable criticism; to Mr. J. Paulin, for the use of the service on the City of God. It illustrates admirably the way in which our worship can spring out of our daily happenings — in this case an afternoon's visit to London — and so all life be hallowed and used sacramentally.

Besides those to whom I know I am indebted for

definite help there are a host to whom I owe what I cannot define. I cannot tell how greatly I am in debt to a home where family prayers were as natural as food, or to the earnest sincerity of him who led them. Or to that vast range of English devotional literature in which Crashaw, Trahern and Andrewes have been my greatest joy. Or to the deep penetration into spiritual relations of Von Hügel, or to the freshness and sacramental insight of that amazing spiritual master Bishop Westcott, or to the present holder of his office at Cambridge, Dr. C. E. Raven, who more than any other has taught me the essential oneness of devotion with "large draughts of intellectual day".

If a book of this kind could have a dedication it would be to Edwin Preece, first student and priest of St Andrew's. It was his use of these prayers in worship that made me accept his suggestion to publish them; and his friendship has encouraged me in the effort to express what far outpasses human thought and speech. Thanks be to God for His unspeakable gift.

N. C. SHERWOOD.

ST. ANDREW'S
WHITTLESFORD.

Notes on the conduct of these services.

The white spaces denote the places where the reader should give a pause for individual thought; only so can the worship move forward as a corporate whole. The wider spaces mark a definite progression in the development of the service.

Hymns should be sung standing unless marked to be sung kneeling. They should not be given out, since there is no need for it, and it spoils the smooth onward flow of the service. All the hymns chosen are familiar ones; a few chords from the pianist, not the playing through of the tune, will be quite sufficient. The starting of the singing needs to be spontaneous and without too big a break. People should be standing before the hymn begins, not get up during the first line.

The numbers given in the services are those in Songs of Praise. A table giving the corresponding numbers in the English Hymnal and in Hymns Ancient and Modern is included. Where these or other books are used it might be well to cross out the number in the text and insert that in the hymn-book used. Exigencies of space make it impossible to print more than one number.

The rest of the service, apart from the canticles, is taken kneeling, unless otherwise indicated. The passages of Scripture want treating as thoughts for meditation rather than as lessons.

The order in which the services are used is left as a matter of choice to the reader.

List of contents.

Foreword
Preface
For preparation before any act of worship
1. The holiness of God
2. The wisdom of God
3. The creative work of God
4. The purpose of God
5. The joy of God
6. Man's expectancy — God's opportunity
7. He ascended into heaven
8. "Tongues like as of flame"
9. The Holy Catholic Church
10. The communion of saints
11. The forgiveness of sins — For meditation
12. The indwelling spirit
13. The renewing of the mind
14. Divine immanence
15. The approach to prayer
16. The city of God — An intercession
17. Preparation for holy communion
18. Our desires — Largely in the nature of meditation
19. The glory that is man's
20. Our faith
Epilogue
Appendix on Drawing up of Services
Acknowledgements
Hymns
Notes

For preparation before any act of worship.

O how amiable are thy dwellings : thou Lord of hosts!

My soul hath a desire and longing to enter into the courts of the Lord : my heart and my flesh rejoice in the living God.

Yea, the sparrow hath found her an house, and the swallow a nest where she may lay her young : even thy altars, O Lord of hosts, my King and my God.

Blessed are they that dwell in thy house : they will be always praising thee.

Blessed is the man whose strength is in thee : in whose heart are thy ways.

Who going through the vale of misery use it for a well : and the pools are filled with water.

They will go from strength to strength : and unto the God of gods appeareth every one of them in Sion.

O Lord God of hosts, hear my prayer : hearken, O God of Jacob.

Behold, O God our defender : and look upon the face of thine Anointed.

For one day in thy courts : is better than a thousand.

I had rather be a doorkeeper in the house of my God : than to dwell in the tents of ungodliness.

For the Lord God is a light and defence : the Lord will give grace and worship, and no good thing shall he withhold from them that live a godly life.

O Lord God of hosts : blessed is the man that putteth his trust in thee.

Or the following thanksgiving by Bishop Andrewes

[*both are worth learning by heart*]

Up with our hearts;
We lift them to the Lord.
O how very meet and right and fitting,
and due,
In all and for all,
At all times, places, manners,
In every season, every spot,
everywhere, always, altogether,
to remember thee, to worship thee,
to confess to thee, to praise thee,
to bless thee, to hymn thee,
To give thanks to thee.
Maker, nourisher, guardian, governor,
preserver, worker, perfecter of all,
Lord and Father,
King and God,
fountain of life and immortality,
treasure of everlasting goods.
Whom the heavens hymn,
and the heavens of heavens,
and angels and all the heavenly powers,
one to other crying continually, —
and we the while, weak and unworthy,
under their feet:—
Holy, Holy, Holy,
Lord the God of Hosts;
full is the whole heaven
and the whole earth
of the majesty of thy glory.
Blessed be the glory of the Lord
out of his place,
for his Godhead, his mysteriousness,
his height, his sovereignty,

his almightiness,
his eternity, his providence.
The Lord is my strength, my stony rock,
and my defence,
my deliverer, my succour, my buckler,
the horn also of my salvation
and my refuge.

1. The holiness of God.

V. O God, thou art my God.
R. Early will I seek thee.

Hymn 187. "Holy, Holy, Holy."

V. Holy, holy, holy is the Lord God of Hosts.
R. The whole earth is full of his Glory.
V. O worship the Lord in the beauty of holiness.
R. Let the whole earth stand in awe of him.

The beauty of the earth cried out, "This is what the whole creation could be, would men but put away the sinful ugliness of their ways one with another. For I, the earth, am the Lord's, and can have no joy nor beauty except in the fulfilment of his purpose. And this my beauty is the sacrament of his passionate caring. His beauty is his holiness pleading with man in love to share his task, his constant work of creation and redemption."

O God, Creator and Father, we praise thee for the marvel of beauty in which thou hast set our lives, for thy love new every morning, shedding upon us the lifegiving power of thy holiness. May we never accept as commonplace the mystery of creation. May the beauty of thy holiness flood our souls, washing away all that is sordid, so that in whatever work our hands shall find this day to do we may show forth something of thy creative power, to thy glory. Amen.

Jesus said: God is Spirit; and they that worship him must worship him in spirit and in truth.

O Lord Christ, who in the perfect reality of thy life hast revealed to us the truth of holiness, Son of Man, Son of God;

> V. Beholding thy courage,
> R. We confess our fear;
> V. Beholding thy sincerity,
> R. We confess our love of convention;
> V. Beholding thy trust in God,
> R. We confess the weakness of our faith;
> V. Beholding thy fulness of life,
> R. We confess our poverty in living.

> O Saviour Christ, thou too art man
> Thou hast been troubled, tempted, tried;
> Thy kind but searching glance can scan
> The very wounds that shame would hide.

The love of God hath been shewn abroad in our hearts by the Spirit of Holiness which was given unto us.

The Holy Ghost shall come upon thee, the power of the most high shall overshadow thee.

Now therefore ye are no more strangers and foreigners, but fellowcitizens with the saints, and of the household of God;

And are built upon the foundation of the apostles and prophets, Jesus Christ himself being the chief corner stone:

In whom all the building fitly framed together groweth into an holy temple in the Lord:

In whom ye also are builded together for an habitation of God through the Spirit.

> Lift up your hearts.
> We lift them up unto the Lord.

With angels and archangels, and all the company of heaven, we laud and magnify thy glorious Name; evermore praising thee and saying [*all together*], Holy, holy, holy, Lord God of hosts, heaven and earth are full of thy glory: Glory be to thee, O Lord most High. Amen.

2. The wisdom of God.

O THE DEPTH OF THE RICHES BOTH OF THE WISDOM AND THE KNOWLEDGE OF GOD! Of him and through him and unto him are all things.

The Lord sitting upon his throne created wisdom,
And poured her out upon all his works.
She is with all flesh according to his gift,
And he gave her freely to them that love him.

With thee, O Lord, is wisdom, which knoweth thy works
And was present when thou wast making the world.
Send her forth out of the holy heavens,
And from the throne of thy glory bid her come;
That being present with me she may toil with me,
That I may learn what is well pleasing before thee.

V. Search me, O God, and know my heart:
R. Try me and know my thoughts:
V. See if I am taking any course of wrong,
R. And lead me in the way everlasting.
V. For with thee is the well of life,
R. And in thy light shall we see light.

CHRIST THE POWER OF GOD AND THE WISDOM OF GOD.
He was made unto us wisdom from God, and righteousness, and redemption, and sanctification.

HYMN 625. "Praise to the Holiest in the height."

Come unto me, all ye that labour and are heavy laden, and I will refresh you.
Take my yoke upon you, and learn from me,

For I am meek and lowly in heart
And ye shall find rest unto your souls.

THE WISDOM THAT IS FROM ABOVE is first pure, then peaceable,
Gentle, easy to be intreated, full of mercy and good fruits,
Without partiality, without hypocrisy.

Fill us, O God, with the knowledge of thy will in all spiritual wisdom and understanding,
That we may walk worthily of thee.
Strengthen us with all power, according to the might of thy glory,
Unto all patience and longsuffering with joy;
So that we may ever give thanks unto thee, who hast delivered us out of the power of darkness,
And translated us in to the kingdom of thy Son, Jesus Christ our Lord. Amen.

BRINGING EVERY THOUGHT INTO CAPTIVITY to the obedience of Christ.
Let the word of Christ dwell in you richly in all wisdom. And whatsoever ye do in word or in deed, do all in the name of the Lord Jesus, giving thanks to God the Father through him.

O Lord, from whom all good things do come; grant to us, thy humble servants, that by thy holy inspiration we may think those things that be good, and by thy merciful guiding may perform the same, through our Lord Jesus Christ. Amen.

The peace of God, which passeth all understanding, shall guard our hearts and our thoughts in Christ Jesus.

3. The creative work of God.

My Father worketh hitherto and I work.

Let us praise God for his creative work in the world of nature.

In the beginning God created the heaven and the earth. And God said, Let there be light: and there was light.

[*Then standing, sing or read antiphonally*]
O all ye works of the Lord: bless ye the Lord,
Praise and exalt him above all for ever,
O ye heavens: bless ye, *etc.*
O ye sun and moon: bless ye, *etc.*
O ye stars of heaven: bless ye, *etc.*
O ye showers and dew: bless ye, *etc.*
O ye winds of God: bless ye, *etc.*
O ye fire and heat: bless ye, *etc.*
O ye frost and cold: bless ye, *etc.*
O ye light and darkness: bless ye, *etc.*
O ye nights and days: bless ye, *etc.*
O ye mountains and hills: bless ye, *etc.*
O ye seas and floods: bless ye, *etc.*
O let the earth now bless the Lord, *etc.*
Gloria.

Let us praise God for his creative work in the creation and redemption of mankind.

We are his workmanship, created in Christ Jesus for good works, which God aforetime prepared that we should walk in them.

Word of God, wisdom of God,
Who wast in the beginning with God,

By whom all worlds were made,
Who bearest on the universe to its appointed goal,
Who art in us the hope of glory
And pledge of ultimate achievement;
In thee we worship the Godhead,
Father, Son and Holy Ghost;
For thou art within us
The Eternal Response and Reason of our being.
Thou for our sakes camest forth from the invisible glory
And wast made man,
Thou didst become what we are
That thou mightest make us what thou art.
For all that thou art to us and in us
How can we ever praise thee?

[*Then standing, again sing*]
O ye children of men: bless ye the Lord, praise and exalt him above all for ever.
O ye priests of the Lord: bless ye, *etc.*
O ye servants o the Lord: bless ye, *etc.*
O ye spirits and souls of the righteous: bless ye, *etc.*
O ye holy and humble men of heart: bless ye, *etc.*
O all ye that worship the Lord: bless ye, *etc.*
Gloria.

My beloved, work out your own salvation with fear and trembling;
For it is God which worketh in you both to will and to work for his good pleasure.

LET US PRAY

Jesus, Master Carpenter, who at the last through wood and nails didst purchase man's whole salvation, wield well thy tools within this thy workshop of our lives, that we who come to thee rough-hewn may by thy hand be fashioned to a truer beauty, for thy glory's sake. Amen.

Now unto him that is able to do exceedingly above all that we ask or think, according to the power that worketh in us, be glory in the Church and in Christ Jesus throughout all ages, world without end. Amen.

4. The purpose of God.

HYMN 300. "God is working his purpose out."

Let us glorify God for the working out of his purpose in days gone by.

*For the way in which in the early centuries of the Church, men were led to perceive with exceeding great clarity the truth of thy Triune Divinity and to formulate their faith in creeds which are still our inspiration.
We worship thee O Lord, and cry aloud,

R.   Hallowed be thy name.

*For the way in which amid the dark ages thou didst send a light to lighten thy people in the conception of the great monastic ideal.
We praise thee,

R.   Praying that thy kingdom come.

For the way in which in our own age thou hast once again visited thy people with the longing to establish thy reign on earth,
We bless thee,

R.   Praying that thy will be done.

For light and life and love moving down the ages, unconquerable, matchless in beauty, drawing men's hearts by the power of truth,
We give thanks to thee, offering ourselves to thee for the service of thy purpose, even as our Master taught us to do, saying,
[*All together*] Our Father, *etc.*

Let us pray for the adventurous spirit in ourselves.
O Thou who art heroic love, keep alive in our hearts

that adventurous spirit, which makes men scorn the way of ease, so that thy will be done. For so only, O Lord, shall we be worthy of those courageous souls, who in every age have ventured in obedience to thy call, and for whom the trumpets have sounded on the other side; through Jesus Christ our Lord. Amen.

Let us pray for the power of perseverance.

O God, who fulfillest thy purpose in unexpected and unimagined ways, speak to us in our hearts when we are baffled, wearied and discouraged, when our minds are darkened by clouds of human misery and crime, and our eyes dimmed by straining for the dawn; remind us that thou hast summed all things in Christ born, crucified, risen, ascended; that in him there lies the fresh spring of wisdom and understanding; that in him nothing is lost, nothing is ineffective, nothing dies but that it may rise to a more fertile life; that in him our least labour becomes a part of the divine ministry. Keep us steadfast, unmovable, always abounding in thy work, knowing that in thee no labour is in vain, and evermore looking for the signs of the coming of thy kingdom of righteousness and peace, which shall be in Jesus Christ our Lord. Amen.

Let us pray [*in silence*] few our own life work, especially for any work we are doing for God just at this time.

Let us rejoice in the kingship of Christ.

Worthy art thou, O Christ, to receive the power, and riches, and wisdom, and might, and honour, and glory, and thanksgiving. For thou wast slain and didst purchase unto God with thy blood men of every tribe, and tongue, and people, and nation, and madest them to be unto our God a kingdom and priests. And they reign upon the earth.

5. The joy of God.

The joy of the Lord is our strength.

At the heart of God is joy.
In thy presence is fulness of joy,
At thy right hand there are pleasures for evermore.

- V. Send out thy light and thy truth that they may lead me;
- R. And bring me to thy holy hill, and to thy dwelling;
- V. That I may go unto the altar of God,
- R. Even unto God my exceeding joy.
- All. Gloria in excelsis deo!

Thou who makest the outgoing of the morning and evening to praise thee, reveal to us thy exceeding joy in creation. Show us wonderful things in thy righteousness, O God of our salvation, thou that art the hope of all the ends of the earth.

Then the Lord answered:—
Where wast thou when I laid the foundations of the earth,
When I created the heavens and stretched them forth,
When the morning stars sang together,
And all the sons of God shouted for joy?

- V. Let the heavens rejoice and let the earth be glad;
- R. Let the sea make a noise and all that therein is.
- V. Let the field be joyful and all that is in it;
- R. Let all the trees of the wood rejoice before

        the Lord.
All.   Gloria in excelsis deo!

Thou, Lord, hast made us glad through thy works, reveal unto us now the exceeding joy of thy strength, that thy people may be joyful and glad in thee.

My thoughts are not your thoughts, neither are your ways my ways, saith the Lord.

And I looked and behold there was a throne set. And I saw in the midst of the throne a Lamb standing that had been slain from the foundation of the world.

V.   Who for the joy that was set before him endured the cross, despising shame;
R.   And is sat down on the right hand of the majesty on high.
V.   Whom not having seen, we love;
R.   In whom we rejoice greatly with joy unspeakable.
All.   Gloria in excelsis deo!

Let us pray

O Christ, who hast made patent for all men the shining pathway through suffering, we thank thee for the pattern of the cross running through all life. O thou who art the true vine, giving thy life for the world, fill us with such a passionate and constant devotion to thee, that our will and our love being attuned unto thine, thy joy may be in us, and our joy be fulfilled, to the glory of thy name. Amen.

O Lord Christ, who being lifted up dost draw all men in their toil and suffering and sin unto thyself:

Grant us so to rejoice in thy light, that we may be mediators of thy joy;

So to share thy life, that we may feed thy sheep;

So to be filled with thy love, that we may heal the world's wounds;

So that all the world may worship thee, sing of thee and praise thy name, saying:

All.   Gloria in excelsis deo!

Hymn 556. "Let all the world in every corner sing."

Now unto him that is able to keep us from falling, and to present us faultless before the presence of his glory with exceeding joy,

To the only wise God our Saviour, be glory and majesty, dominion and power, both now and for ever. Amen.

6. Man's expectancy — God's opportunity.

I. The Anticipation

Yet a very little time and he that cometh shall come and shall not tarry.

I will stand upon my watch and set me upon the tower, and will look forth to see what he will speak with me, and what I shall answer.

And the Lord answered me and said, Write the Vision, and make it plain upon tablets, that he may run that readeth it.

For the Vision is yet for the appointed time, and it hasteth toward the end, and shall not lie;

Though it tarry, wait for it;

Because it will surely come, it will not delay.

V. My soul, be thou silent unto God.
R. For my expectation is from him.

[*After a pause of silence, the following to be said antiphonally or preferably sung to a chant. Remain kneeling.*]

> How beautiful upon the mountains
> Are the feet of him, that publisheth peace,
> That bringeth good tidings of good;
> That saith unto Zion, Thy God reigneth.
>
> The voice of thy watchmen! They lift up their voice

And together do sing.
For they shall see eye to eye
When the Lord returneth to Zion.

Break forth in joy, sing together,
Ye wasted places of Jerusalem;
For the Lord hath comforted his people
He hath redeemed Jerusalem

The Lord hath made bare his holy arm
In the eyes of all the nations
And all the ends of the earth
Shall see the salvation of our God.

II. The Vision

A woman when she is in travail hath sorrow, because her hour is come: but when she is delivered of the child she remembereth no more the anguish for joy that a man is born unto the world.

> Hymn 79. "O little town of Bethlehem."

Unto us a child is born;
Unto us a son is given;
And the government shall be upon his shoulder.
They shall call his name Immanuel, God with us.
He shall save his people from their sins.

III. The Thanksgiving

[*All standing*]

Simeon received the child into his arms and blessed God and said:

[*To be sung or said by all*]
Lord, now lettest thou servant depart in peace,
According to thy word.
For mine eyes have seen thy salvation,
Which thou has prepared
Before the face of all people;
To be a light to lighten the Gentiles,
And to be the glory of thy people Israel.
Gloria.

IV. The Resolution

[*All kneeling*]

The earnest expectation of the creation
Waiteth for the revealing of the sons of God.

7. He ascended into heaven.

Who for the joy that was set before him endured the cross, despising the shame, and hath sat down on the right hand of the throne of God.

O Lord Jesus Christ, whom not having seen, we love; on whom, though we see thee not, yet believing, we rejoice greatly with joy unspeakable and full of glory; We give thanks to thee for they great victory and power, whereby we know that sin no longer hath the dominion, but that thou art Ruler in the kingdoms of men. Praise be to thee, our Lord and king, for ever. Amen.

[*Then may be said by all together, standing*]

Glory to thee, O Christ our ascended and ever present Lord, through whom we have access to the Father.
Glory to thee who lovest us and hast loosed us from our sins.
Glory to thee who hast reconciled us all in one body unto God through thy cross, so that we are no more strangers and sojourners but fellowcitizens with the saints in the household of God.
Glory to thee who dost redeem unto God with thy blood men of every title and tongue and people and nation.
Glory to thee who art with us always, even unto the end of the world.
Glory to thee who art in our midst when we are gathered together in thy name.
Glory to thee, the author and finisher of our faith, that God in all things may be glorified.

Amen.

Let us pray

O God the king of glory, who hast exalted thine only Son Jesus Christ with great triumph unto thy kingdom in heaven; we beseech thee, leave us not comfortless; but send to us thine Holy Ghost to comfort us, and exalt us unto the same place whither our Saviour Christ is gone before, who liveth and reigneth with thee and the Holy Ghost, one God, world without end. Amen.

Hymn 632. "Rejoice, the Lord is King."

God hath spoken unto us in his Son, whom he appointed heir of all things, through whom also he made the worlds; who, upholding all things by the word of his power, when he had made purification of sins, sat down on the right hand of the Majesty on high.

Christ entered not into a holy place made with hands, but into heaven itself, now to appear before the face of God for us.

Jesus said, All authority hath been given unto me in heaven and on earth. Go ye into all the world, and preach the gospel to the whole creation.

O God the Father, who hast highly exalted thy Son Jesus Christ and given unto him the name which is above every name; grant us so to see the vision of his splendour and become partakers of his humility that we may go forth boldly to the proclamation of his kingdom. Hasten, we pray thee, the day when in his name, in whom the worlds were made, every knee shall bow, and every tongue confess him Lord; to thy glory, O Eternal Father, who with the Son and Holy Ghost livest and reignest one God blessed for evermore. Amen.

May all the peoples from the rising of the sun even unto the going down of the same cry aloud in praise to thee with joyful voice and say, Glory to thee, O God, the Saviour of all, forever. Amen.

At Whitsuntide

8. "Tongues like as of flame."

Let us pray that the enkindling fire of God may come upon his Church.

Almighty God, our heavenly Father, whose Son Jesus Christ came to cast fire upon the earth; grant that by the prayers of thy faithful people a fire of burning zeal may pass from heart to heart, till all our hardness is melted in the warmth of thy love; through him who loved us and gave himself for us, the same Jesus Christ our Lord. Amen.

Let us pray for the cleansing fire to work in our own lives.

O thou who art refiner's fire to purge away the dross, and prunest the branches of thy vine that they may bear the more fruit; give us thy grace that we may come bravely to the light, and not fear what thy holy love shall do in us. In patience may we possess our souls, knowing that thou dealest with us as sons, that we may be to the praise of thy glory in Jesus Christ our Lord. Amen.

Who maketh his ministers a flame of fire.

The Veni Creator. [*Kneeling. To be said or sung.*]

> Come, Holy Ghost, our souls inspire,
> And lighten with celestial fire.
> Thou the anointing Spirit art,
> Who dost thy seven-fold gifts impart.
>
> Thy blessed Unction from above.

Is comfort, life and fire of love.
Enable with perceptual light
The dullness of our blinded sight.

Anoint and cheer our soiled face
With the abundance of thy grace.
Keep far our foes, give peace at home!
Where thou art guide, no ill can come.

Teach us to know the Father, Son,
And thee, of both, to be but One.
That, through the ages all along,
This may be our endless song;
    Praise to thy eternal merit,
    Father, Son and Holy Spirit.

Lord of the ages who makest thy messengers spirits, and thy servants a flame of fire; stir up, we pray thee, thy gift in all stewards of thy mysteries, that thy Word may flash forth as the lightning from one corner of the heavens unto the other. Baptise thy Church with the Holy Spirit and the consuming fire of thy love, and cause her light to shine as a city set on a hill; that all mankind may see her steadfast and glorious light, and draw near to worship thee in the unity of the body of thy Son Jesus Christ. Amen.

HYMN 211. "Disposer Supreme."

Defend, O Lord, us thy servants with thy heavenly grace, that we may continue thine for ever; and daily increase in thy Holy Spirit more and more, till we come to thine everlasting kingdom. Amen.

9. The Holy Catholic Church.

> The Church's one foundation is
> Jesus Christ our Lord.

Hymn 249. "The Church's one foundation."

Let us pray for the illumination of the Church.

O God, the Father of glory, give unto thy Church a spirit of wisdom and revelation in the knowledge of thee; enlighten the eyes of our heart, that we may know what is the hope of our calling, what the riches of the glory of thy inheritance in the saints, what the exceeding greatness of thy power which wrought in Christ, and gave him to be head over all things to thy Church, his body, the fulness of him that filleth all in all. Amen.

I was in the spirit on the Lord's day, and I heard behind me a great voice. And I turned to see the voice which spake with me. And having turned, I saw seven golden candlesticks; and in the midst one like unto a Son of man. His eyes were as a flame of fire; and his voice as the voice of many waters. And he had in his right hand seven stars: and out of his mouth proceeded a sharp two-edged sword; and his countenance was as the sun shineth in his strength.

These things saith he that holdeth the seven stars in his right hand:—

I know thy works, and thy toil, and patience; but I have this against thee, that thou didst leave thy first love. Remember, therefore, from whence thou art fallen, and repent, and do the first works.

To him that overcometh will I give to eat of the tree

of life.

 V. He that hath an ear, let him hear
 R. What the Spirit saith unto the Churches.

These things saith the first and the last which was dead and is alive again:—

I know thy tribulation and thy poverty, but thou art rich. Fear not the things which thou must suffer. Be thou faithful unto death, and I will give thee the crown of life.

He that overcometh shall not be hurt of the second death.

 V.&R. He that hath, *etc.*

These things saith he that hath the sharp two-edged sword:—

I know where thou dwellest, even where evil sits enthroned; and thou holdest fast my name.

To him that overcometh I will give a white stone, and upon the stone a new name written, which no one knoweth but he that receiveth it.

 V.&R. He that hath, *etc.*

These things saith the Son of God whose eyes are like a flame of fire:—

All the churches shall know that I am he which searcheth the reins and hearts: and I will give unto each one of you according to your works.

To him that overcometh will I give the morning star.

 V.&R. He that hath, *etc.*

These things saith he that hath the seven spirits of God:—

Be thou watchful and stablish the things that remain, which were ready to die.

If thou shalt not watch, I will come as a thief, and

thou shalt not know what hour I will come upon thee.

He that overcometh shall be arrayed in white garments; and I will confess his name before my Father, and before his Angels.

V.&R.   He that hath, *etc.*

These things saith the faithful and true witness, the beginning of the creation of God:-

Thou sayest, I am rich, and have need of nothing; and knowest not that thou art wretched and poor and blind and naked.

I counsel thee to buy of me gold refined by fire, and white garments, and eye salve to anoint thine eyes that thou mayest see. As many as I love I reprove and chasten.

He that overcometh, I will give to him to sit down with me on my throne, as I also overcame and sat down with my Father in his throne.

V.&R.   He that hath, *etc.*

These things saith he that is holy, he that is true, he that openeth, and no man shutteth:—

Behold, I have set before thee a door opened, which no one can shut.

He that overcometh, I will make him a pillar in the sanctuary of my God, and he shall go out thence no more.

V.&R.   He that hath, *etc.*

Let us pray for the unity of the Church.

O God the Father, Origin of Divinity, Good beyond all that is good, fair beyond all that is fair, in whom is calmness, peace and concord; do thou make up the dissensions which divide us from each other, and bring us back into an unity of love which may bear some likeness to thy Divine nature, revealed unto us by the Holy Ghost in Jesus Christ our Lord. Amen.

Let us pray for all leaders of the Church.

O God, who before the passion of thine only begotten Son didst reveal thy glory upon the holy mount; Grant unto thy servants that in faith beholding the light of his countenance, they may be strengthened to bear his cross, and be changed into his likeness, from glory to glory; through the same Jesus our Lord. Amen.

Let us pray for the life of the whole Church.

O God of unchangeable power and eternal light, look favourably on on thy whole Church, that wonderful and sacred mystery; and by the tranquil operation of thy perpetual providence carry out the work of man's salvation, and let the whole world feel and see that things that were cast down are being raised up; that those things which had grown old are being made new; and that all things are moving towards perfection, through him for whom they took their origin, even Jesus Christ our Lord. Amen.

Christ loved the Church, and gave himself up for it; that he might sanctify it, having cleansed it by the washing of water with the word, that he might present the Church to himself a glorious Church, not having spot, or wrinkle, or any such thing; but that it should be holy and without blemish, his body, the fulness of him that filleth all in all.

10. The communion of saints

The Church is the fellowship of his body. The Communion of Saints is the inner relationship of the members of that body. It implies a deep interdependence, a natural drawing together of those who for Christ's sake have chosen the way of consecration.

Let us thank God for those who in every age have seen the vision of consecration and fellowship and have drawn others into it.

For the multitude which no man can number, gathered out of every nation and kindred and people and tongue.

V.   We praise thee,
R.   We give thanks to thee.

That we are all knit in the one communion and fellowship in Thy Son,

V.&R.   We praise thee, *etc.*

For all holy and humble men of heart, who have followed thee in quiet, unseen ways,

V.&R.   We praise thee, *etc.*

For all who for thy sake have borne labour and poverty, anguish, persecution and the sword,

V.&R.   We praise thee, *etc.*

For those, the known and unknown, through whom the gospel came to our land,

V.&R.   We praise thee, *etc.*

For all clear souls through whom we have seen the light,

V.&R. We praise thee, *etc.*

For the sacraments of thy love, whereby we are knit into one body,

V.&R. We praise thee, *etc.*

Above all, we praise thee for our Elder Brother, firstborn among many brethren; That he is not ashamed to call us brethren,

V.&R. We praise thee, *etc.*

That he took our nature upon him and was made man,

V.&R. We praise thee, *etc.*

That by death he has brought to nought the separating power of death, and delivered all who through fear of death were all their life subject to bondage,

V.&R. We praise thee, *etc.*

That he is with us always, even unto the end of the age,

V.&R. We praise thee, *etc.*

Jesus prayed saying:
Sanctify them through thy truth: thy word is truth.
As thou hast sent me into the world, even so have I also sent them into the world.
And for their sakes I sanctify myself, that they also might be sanctified through the truth.
Neither pray I for these alone, but for them also which shall believe on me through their word;
That they all may be one; as thou, Father, art in me, and I in thee, that they also may be one in us: that the world may believe that thou hast sent me.

Let us seek that consecration individually for ourselves as and as a fellowship. [*All together say this confession*]

O King and Christ, ruling over us by the majesty of thy fearless love, we confess to thee

The pettiness of the ambitions which have held us;

The tawdriness of the successes we have worshipped;

The domination that fear of pain and failure has held over us.

Save us, we pray thee,
    From all self-regarding schemes,
    All desires for comfort of body and soul,
    All conceit in our own attainments.

O thou Captain of our salvation,
By love make us selfless;
Unite us to thee in thy dying,
So that we may be set free, in the power of thy Resurrection,
To tread the road of true achievement,
To the fulfilling of the eternal purposes of God.
Amen.

O thou almighty Spirit of God, energy of God, overshadow us with thy divine power; enable us for the task awaiting us, even the renewing of this thy world.

Give us the vision of a whole united human family, and the patience to work on humbly and consistently to that end. Teach us the splendour of love. Endue us with thy divine courtesy which never over-rides; open our eyes to see thee at work in our brethren; and may we in love and joy give ourselves to their service, for the sake of Him who gave himself for us, even Jesus Christ our Lord. Amen.

God the Father, who didst make of one blood all

men to dwell on the face of the earth,

God the Son, who hast made us one by the blood of thy Cross,

God the Holy Ghost, in whom alone we abide one body,

We praise thee that neither race nor language, wealth nor poverty, learning nor ignorance can put asunder those whom thou hast joined together, that all are one in thee with those who have gone before and with the generations yet to come, one man growing up into thee, O Christ, who art the head of the body, and fillest all in all. Amen.

Ye are come unto mount Sion, and unto the city of the living God, the heavenly Jerusalem, and to an innumerable company of angels,

To the general assembly and church of the firstborn, which are written in heaven, and to God the Judge of all, and to the spirits of just men made perfect.

HYMN 202. "For all the Saints."

Therefore let us also, seeing we are compassed about with so great a cloud of witnesses, lay aside every weight, and the sin which doth so easily beset us, and let us run with patience the race that is set before us,

Looking unto Jesus.

11. The forgiveness of sins — For meditation.

[*This Meditation grew out of consideration of a gospel incident. One of the most fruitful methods of meditation is to take some story and put oneself into the place of each of the various actors or groups of actors in turn. If we are to progress in the knowledge of God and fulfilment of his will we must ever keep before us the twofold question, "Who is God, who am I?" By putting ourselves into the position of the characters of a gospel story we gain an ever-deepening insight into the answer, as we watch as it were, from the angle of those present, the impact Jesus makes on those around him. Before reading the Meditation, HYMN 666, "There's a wideness in God's mercy," could be sung.*]

Luke vii. 36-50.

Jesus is in the house of Simon the Pharisee with the woman of notoriety weeping over his feet. We see him evoking response, drawing people into contact with himself. It is not only the woman. Simon has been sufficiently attracted to desire the presence of Jesus with himself and his friends.

And this is the first fact about God. God attracts, God evokes from man response. God wakes an echo in the heart of Simon as well as in the heart of the woman. God finds us and claims a kinship with us. That is the first fact about God.

Within the contact he has made Jesus begins his creative work. There can be no more perfect example than this story of the meaning of forgiveness of sins.

The woman has gone wrong because she has used her great power of self-giving on the physical level. Jesus sees in her this power. It is to him of far more importance than her sin. He takes hold of it, and out of the instrument of her degradation fashions the implement of her redemption. Her sins which are many are forgiven, for she loved much. There it is, this faculty of self-giving, used on the lowest level to make a ready means of livelihood, degraded and despised. Jesus, the supreme revealer of God, in his creative originality, finding that very quality in all its rags and dirt, lifts it up to the place it should occupy, causing it to be the king of her soul, a deep, outgoing, creative, redemptive love.

That is the second fact about God; that is what God is like, that is what he does, him whom we call Father, that is his quality of creative originality.

In the house of Simon are his friends, those that sat at meat and raised the questioning about forgiveness, some of the followers of Jesus too, Jesus in the midst and the woman. With which of these can we take our place? Consider each in turn.

The woman. No; I suppose we don't fit in there, probably because we are not any of us big enough, having sinned on such a scale to make so magnificent an act of contrition, or to win so superb an experience of forgiveness. The woman knows well enough that hostile eyes are round her. Her action isn't mere Eastern exuberance. She knows what the men will think of her, she knows her shame, but she passes beyond it all because she cares for Jesus. What does it matter what they say or think, how they jeer, how odd it seems? She knows only her need of Jesus and his redeeming quality. At last she has found someone big enough to understand even in its crudest form all she has to give.

Simon. Surely we should not have behaved as he did; we should have been more understanding. Is that really so? Simon, after all, has invited in this strange unorthodox teacher to meet his own friends. Are we ready to understand the new, the unaccepted, that which is not within our own particular ecclesiastical system? Simon was discourteous in that he showed Jesus none of the customary civilities of hospitality. Are we always courteous to the folk we consider our inferiors? "Inasmuch as ye did it not unto one of the least of these, ye did it not unto me."

Simon's friends. Greatly we hope not to have to take our place among them, the people who have enough interest to come and see this new phenomenon but sit back, detached, unable to appreciate the miracle before their eyes. God grant we be not of those who narrow the divine goodness down to the channels of their own pet orthodoxy.

The disciples of Jesus. It sounds more comfortable at first sight to find ourselves among them. But what part do we play here? Simon leans over to us and says, "Can't you look after this master of yours better, why do you let riff-raff follow him about? Is it quite fair on me, when I have asked these friends of mine to meet him, to let this woman turn up and make an exhibition of herself?" What do we answer? Don't we feel ashamed under his criticism; isn't there after all something to be said for his position? Isn't this at best a non-committal answer we are murmuring? We do find it so difficult to mix with men, entering into all that is good and wholesome in their life, yet not for one instant allowing our own conduct to be regulated by any other standard than the highest. It is often a very dangerous place to be amongst the friends of Jesus. It is the place that so easily and so swiftly leads to denial.

Jesus. Is this the real answer to our question, who am I, that the only place where we truly belong, even we with all our faults, is the place of Jesus himself? "As I am, so are ye in this world." Is that true? Then it means that there is in this situation and in Jesus' conduct of it nothing inherently impossible for us to achieve.

We must begin then as Jesus began to win folk. We can only do it by winning them to what they discover of God in us, to our highest selves. The world can't be saved by philosophy; person can only be won to person.

No shyness must hinder us. Jesus was not for one moment embarrassed by the woman's conduct, nor is he ever afraid or ashamed to be the central figure in a situation, for he is bringing men God, and the place for God is in the centre of life.

The power to forgive, that too is given us, to reach down into the sin of folk and find there the very thing that can work their redemption through our faith in them, our love for them.

We can hardly bear it, the sight of what we are meant to be, what we might be, and what we are. But he who as Son eternally makes response to the Father is prepared to make that response from within us. "That which Jesus gives to those who are his is himself, the very essence of his thought, his faith, his heart. He gives himself without stint to kindle in them the flame which consumes him, to bring to birth and maintain in each one of them the hope and energy and certainty which animate him."

12. The indwelling spirit.

Thus saith the high and lofty One, that inhabiteth eternity, whose name is Holy; I dwell in the high and holy place, with him also that is of a contrite and humble spirit, to revive the spirit of the humble, and to revive the heart of the contrite ones.

O Holy Spirit of God, creator Spirit, renew in us a contrite heart. Show us the poverty of our ideals, the dullness of our thoughts of thee, the lethargy that besets us when we should be striving with joy to establish thy kingdom. Create in us a clean heart, O God, and renew a steadfast spirit in us. Cast us not away from thy presence, but restore unto us the joy of thy salvation, and uphold us with a free and willing spirit; for thy name's sake. Amen.

As many as are led by the Spirit of God, these are the sons of God. Ye received not the spirit of bondage unto fear; but ye received the spirit of adoption, whereby we cry, Abba, Father. The Spirit himself beareth witness with our spirit, that we are children of God. And if children, then heirs; heirs of God, and joint-heirs with Christ; if so be that we suffer with him, that we may also be glorified with him.

O Spirit of the living Christ, ever bearing the sin and sorrow of the world, yet triumphant over death itself, dwell in us and make us unafraid to claim our sonship, even though it lead us to the cross. Amen.

The Father will give you another Comforter, even the spirit of truth; ye know him, for he abideth with you, and shall be in you.

He that abideth in love abideth in God, and God abideth in him.

> O little lark, you need not fly
> To seek your master in the sky,
> He treads our native sod;
> Why should you sing aloft, apart?
> Sing to the heaven of my heart;
> In me, in me, in me is God!
>
> O little lark, sing loud and long
> To Him who gave you flight and song,
> And me a heart aflame.
> He loveth them of low degree,
> And he hath magnified me,
> And holy, holy, holy is his name!

Steadfast I worship, for Thou art so near me—
Set in a soul, my one Holy of Holies.

Hymn 573. "Love divine."

Let us pray

O God our Father,
From whom every family in heaven and on earth is named,
Grant us, according to the riches of thy glory,
That we may be strengthened with power through thy spirit in the inward man;
That Christ may dwell in our hearts by faith;
To the end that we being rooted and grounded in love,
May be strong to apprehend, with all the saints

What is the breadth and length and height and depth,
And to know the love of Christ
Which passeth knowledge,
That we may be filled even with all thy fulness
In Christ our Lord. Amen.

13. The renewing of the mind.

Be ye renewed in the spirit of your mind,
And be not fashioned according to this world.

> I saw the Son of God go by
>   Crowned with the crown of Thorn.
> "Was it not finished, Lord?" I said,
>   "And all the anguish borne?"
> He turned on me his awful eyes:
>   "Hast thou not understood?
> Lo! Every soul is Calvary,
>   And every sin a Rood."

LET US PRAY

Lord, have mercy upon us,
Christ, have mercy upon us,
Lord, have mercy upon us.

From traditionalism and acceptance of this world's standards,
From want of faith in the sure accomplishment of thy purpose,
From all anger, contempt, and indifference,

V.   By the coming of the Holy Ghost
R.   Good Lord, deliver us.

From self-deceiving and complacency,
From hardness, narrowness and distrust,
From ignorance and lighthearted foolishness,

V.   By the coming of the Holy Ghost
R.   Good Lord, deliver us.

From sloth and lack of perseverance,
From lazy choosing of the easier, less good ways,
From failure in love, and from keeping back part of the cost,

    V.   By the coming of the Holy Ghost
    R.   Good Lord, deliver us.

By thine agony and bloody sweat,
By thy cross and passion,
By thy precious death and burial,
By thy glorious Resurrection and Ascension,

    V.   And by the coming of the Holy Ghost
    R.   Good Lord, deliver us.

By the dumb anguish of thy suffering world,
By thy renewed crucifixion in the secret places of our souls,
By the daily travail of thy love for us,

    V.   And by the coming of the Holy Ghost
    R.   Good Lord, deliver us.

Be ye transformed, by the renewing of your mind.
By his mercy he saved us, through the washing of regeneration and the renewing of the Holy Ghost, which he poured out upon us richly through Jesus Christ our Saviour.

[*Sung kneeling*] HYMN 180. "Come, thou holy Paraclete."

Almighty and ever living God, who hast vouchsafed to regenerate us thy servants by water and the Holy Ghost, and hast given unto us forgiveness of all our sins; strengthen us, we beseech thee, O Lord, with the Holy Ghost the Comforter, and daily increase in us thy manifold gifts of grace; the spirit of wisdom and understanding, the spirit of counsel and ghostly strength, the spirit of knowledge and true godliness; and fill us, O Lord, with the spirit of thy holy fear, now and evermore. Amen.

I will put a new spirit within you, and ye shall be my people, and I will be your God.

If any man is in Christ, there is a new creation.

Our inward man is renewed day by day, after the image of him that created him; that we might prove what is that good, and acceptable, and
          Perfect, will of God.

14. Divine immanence.

> Master, where abidest thou?
> He saith unto them, Come and ye shall see.
> They came therefore and saw where he abode,
> And they abode with him.
>
> They constrained him, saying, Abide with us: for it is toward evening, and the day is now far spent. And he went in to abide with them.
> And it came to pass, when he had sat down to meat, he took the bread and blessed it, and brake, and gave to them.
> And their eyes were opened, and they knew him; and he was known of them in the breaking of bread.

I come in the little things,
Saith the Lord:
Not borne on morning wings
Of majesty, but I have set My Feet
Amidst the delicate and bladed wheat
That springs triumphant in the furrowed sod.
There do I dwell, in weakness and in power;
Not broken or divided, saith our God!
In your straight garden plot I come to flower:
About your porch My Vine
Meek, fruitful, doth entwine;
Waits, at the threshold, Love's appointed hour.

I come in the little things,
Saith the Lord:
Yea! on the glancing wings
Of eager birds, the softly pattering feet
Of furred and gentle beasts, I come to meet
Your hard and wayward heart. In brown bright eyes

That peep from out the brake, I stand confest.
On every nest
Where feathery Patience is content to brood
And leaves her pleasure for the high emprize
Of motherhood—
There doth My Godhead rest.

I come in the little things,
Saith the Lord:
My starry wings
I do forsake,
Love's highway of humility to take:
Meekly I fit my stature to your need.
In beggar's part
About your gates I shall not cease to plead—
As man, to speak with man—
Till by such art
I shall achieve My Immemorial Plan,
Pass the low lintel of the human heart.

Behold, I stand at the door and knock; if any man hear my voice and open the door, I will come in to him, and will sup with him, and he with me.

Enter, Lord, the dwelling place of our heart and take possession of us, of all we are and all we have, for in humility and joy we offer ourselves to thee. Lord, thou knowest that for all our failings we love thee. Speak to us of thy great purposes for men, and breathe into us thy divine longings, so that by thy communing with us we may be made strong to serve thee in our fellows, feed thy lambs, seek thy lost sheep. And grant, O Lord, that the door of our life may ever be set so wide open to thee that, whatever be the manner of thy coming we may be quick to know thy footfall, and bring to thee the glad adoration that we offer thee now, our Saviour for evermore. Amen.

If any man love me, he will keep my word: and my Father will love him, and we will come unto him and make our abode with him.

V. He that heareth, let him say, Come.
R. Amen, Come Lord Jesus.

The grace of the Lord Jesus Christ be with all the Saints. Amen.

15. The approach to prayer.

    V.   When thou saidst, Seek ye my face, my heart said unto thee:
    R.   Thy face, Lord, will I seek.
    V.   With my whole heart have I sought thee.

THE APPROACH OF EARNEST EXPECTATION.

O God, thou art my God, I yearn for thee,
Body and soul, I thirst, I long for thee,
Like a barren and dry land where no water is.

Thy love is more than life to me,
So my lips shall praise thee,
My soul be richly fed,
My mouth praise thee with joyful lips.

When I remember thee upon my bed,
And meditate on thee in the night watches,
My soul clings fast to thee,
For thou hast been my help,
And in the shadow of thy wings will I rejoice.

    V.   O thou that hearest prayer,
    R.   Unto thee shall all flesh come.

THE APPROACH OF QUIET LISTENING.

He wakeneth morning by morning,
He wakeneth mine ear to hear as they that are taught.
I will hear what God the Lord will speak;
For he shall speak peace unto his people,
And unto his saints.

After the fire a voice of gentle stillness. And Elijah wrapped his face in his mantle and went out, and stood in the entering in of the cave.

    V.   Thou has made us for thyself, and our hearts are restless,
    R.   Until they find their rest in thee.

Refresh us, O God, with the vision of thy Being and Beauty, that in the joy of thy strength we may work without haste and without sloth, through Jesus Christ our Lord. Amen.

The approach of personal consecration.

Return unto thy rest, O my soul,
For the Lord hath dealt bountifully with thee.
What shall I render unto the Lord
For all his benefits toward me?
I will take the cup of salvation,
And call upon the name of the Lord.

If I regard iniquity in my heart,
The Lord will not hear me.
O Lord, truly I am thy servant.
I will offer to thee the sacrifice of thanksgiving.
Let the lifting up of my hands be as the evening sacrifice.

[*To be sung kneeling*] Hymn 458. "Breathe on me, breath of God."

Lord, Teach us to Pray.

And Jesus said unto them, When ye pray, say [*all*

together]

> Our Father,
> Which art in heaven,
> Hallowed be thy name.
> Thy kingdom come,
> Thy will be done
> On earth, as it is in heaven.
> Give us this day our daily bread,
> And forgive us our trespasses
> As we forgive them that trespass against us,
> And lead us not into temptation,
> But deliver us from evil;
> For thine is the kingdom, the power and the glory,
> For ever and ever. Amen.

16. The city of God — An intercession.

Great is the Lord and highly to be praised in the city of our God.

I. The Vision.

Let us give thanks to our Father and King for the vision of the splendid city.

O God our Father, we humbly thank thee that through the Incarnation of thy Son has been given to us the vision of this earth as the Kingdom of God, and through his death has been made plain to us the way of sacrifice, whereby the cities of this world may become the cities of the Eternal King. Keep bright, O God, that vision ever before our eyes, and give us wisdom and strength to work continually for its achievement; that thy glory may cover the earth in Christ our Lord. Amen.

Let us confess to God that having been given the vision, we have often betrayed it.

O Lord God, we have sinned and dealt wickedly, turning aside from thy precepts and judgements; we have sinned by class injustice, by indifference to the sufferings of the poor, by want of true patriotism, by greed and secret self-seeking. Turn then our hearts, O God, that we may truly repent and utterly abhor the manifold evils which our sins have brought upon this and other nations. Break down our idols of pride and wealth, scatter our self-love, open our eyes to see that daily life and public work must be consecrated to the building of that city which hath the foundations in

Jesus Christ our Lord. Amen.

II. The Work.

We thank thee, O Lord, for the measure in which men's minds have responded to the building of thy city; for the heritage of the past in great buildings and noble traditions, for the growing concern for human life and the care of little children. Give us a kindling enthusiasm to take our share in the task, for the sake of him who went about doing good, even thy son Jesus Christ the Saviour of men. Amen.

We pray thee to take from us all acquiescence in the continuance of slums and bless the efforts of all who are striving to remove them.

V. O Lord, hear our prayer.
R. And let our cry come unto thee.

Grant that all who build our cities may have a concern for beauty without which men's souls starve;

V. O Lord, hear our prayer.
R. And let our cry come unto thee.

That provision may be made for open spaces, where children may play, and the weary rest in the shadow of trees,

V. O Lord, hear our prayer.
R. And let our cry come unto thee.

That the life of our cities may be enriched by opportunities for music, art and drama,

V. O Lord, hear our prayer.
R. And let our cry come unto thee.

That thou wilt bless all who labour to banish

disease, and teach men to respect their bodies.

V.　　O Lord, hear our prayer.
R.　　And let our cry come unto thee.

That thou wilt save those who are ready to sell their souls for the meat that perisheth, revealing to them that a man's life consisteth not in the abundance of the things he possesseth.

V.　　O Lord, hear our prayer.
R.　　And let our cry come unto thee.

III. The Choice.

The End of the City of Mammon

Woe, woe, the great city Babylon, the strong city! for in one hour is thy judgement come.

And the merchants of the earth shall weep and mourn over her; for no man buyeth their merchandise any more;

The merchandise of gold, and silver, and precious stones, and of pearls, and fine linen, and purple, and silk, and scarlet;

And cinnamon, and odours, and ointments, and frankincense, and wine, and oil, and fine flour, and wheat, and beasts, and merchandise of horses and chariots, and slaves, and souls of men.

Woe, woe, the great city, wherein were made rich all that had ships in the sea by reason of her costliness! for in one hour is she made desolate.

The Coming of the City of God

And I saw the holy city, new Jerusalem, coming

down out of heaven from God, prepared as a bride adorned for her husband.

And I heard a great voice out of heaven saying, Behold, the tabernacle of God is with men, and he shall dwell with them, and they shall be his people, and God himself shall be with them, and be their God.

And God shall wipe away all tears from their eyes; and there shall be no more death, neither sorrow, nor crying, neither shall there be any more pain: for the former things are passed away.

Hymn 468. "City of God, how broad and far."

Beautiful in elevation, the joy of the whole earth is the city of the Great King. Let thy work appear unto thy servants, and thy glory upon their children; and may the beauty of the Lord our God be upon us. Establish thou the work of our hands upon us; yea, the work of our hands, establish thou it. Amen.

17. Preparation for holy communion.

It is our duty to render most humble and hearty thanks to Almighty God our heavenly Father, for he hath given his Son our Saviour, Jesus Christ, not only to die for us, but also to be our spiritual food and sustenance in the holy Sacrament of the Body and Blood of Christ.

Blessed art thou, O God and Father of our Lord Jesus Christ; Thou hast blessed us with every spiritual blessing in Christ.
Thou didst choose us in him before the foundation of the world; to be holy and without blemish before thee in love.
Thou hast foreordained us unto adoption as sons through Jesus Christ unto thyself, according to the good pleasure of thy will,
That we should be to the praise of the glory of thy grace, which thou hast freely bestowed on us in the Beloved;
In whom we have our redemption through his blood;
The forgiveness of our sins,
According to the riches of thy grace.

[*By all together, quietly and slowly*] All this hast thou done for us, O God our Father, but we have forgotten thee. Thou hast opened to us the unsearchable riches of our Lord Christ, but we have chosen to live beggarly. Thou hast put thy Holy Spirit within us to lead us, but we have gone our own earthly way. Always we have been more interested in ourselves than in thee. O Lord, forgive our trespasses, as we forgive them that trespass against us. Set us free from the worship of ourselves, that it may be our meat and drink to do thy will. Amen.

Blessed be thy name, O Lord God, who hast set before us life and death, and hast bidden us choose life.

Behold, O Lord, with all our heart we choose life; we choose thee, O God, for thou art our life. Save, Lord, and hear us, O king of heaven, and accept the sacrifice of our whole heart which now we give to thee.

O Lord our God, we offer thee our senses and passions, and all our faculties;

All our desires, all our designs, all our studies, all our endeavours;

All the remainder of our life.

All that we have or are we offer up entirely to thy service.

Lord, sanctify us wholly, that our whole spirit, soul, and body may become thy temple. O do thou dwell in us, and be thou our God, and we will be thy servants for ever and ever. Amen.

<small>The prayer of the four voices.</small>

They shall come from the East and from the West, from the North and from the South, and sit down in the Kingdom of God.

[Each of these four prayers may well be read by a different voice]

<small>The prayer of the North.</small>
[Memorial.]

The bitter bleakness of my northern clime

By the memorial of thy bitter death
Thaw, and bow down my stubborn pride,
My self-sufficiency, that springs from fear
Of loving thee so much that I forget
To be a man.

THE PRAYER OF THE SOUTH.
[Eucharist.]

With joy ecstatic of the southern skies
And brilliant gladness of thanksgiving noon,
My Christ, my king, I hasten to thy feast.
As the great dawn sweeps up the flanks
Of spectral darkness, breaking up the night,
So flash thy strong beams searchingly
Through all the habitations of my mind,
Driving out superstition, lust, and pride,
That I may stand, thy worshipper, with hands
Upraised to praise thee, and outstretched to bless.

THE PRAYER OF THE WEST.
[Communion.]

In multitudes we come, one holy fellowship
Close knit by thine activity of love,
To work and pray, and be thy very body
Indwelt and used, how, when and where
We best may serve thee, Son of Man, who know

That prayer and work are one.

The prayer of the East.
[Sacrifice.]

>Eternal Son of God, by whom all worlds
>Were called in being, day-star from on high,
>Age-old we guard for thee earth's mystery,
>Of life in death, gain hammered out of loss,
>Slow on the tear scorched anvil of heart's pain.
>Thy costly sacrifice irradiates the world,
>Gives man his answer perfect to thy call.
>All lesser gifts, transformed, made one in thee,
>Bring timelessness to succour time's vast need.
>Lord of our hearts—
>Words break, but thy sufficiency holds strong
>The passionate comprehension of our souls.

Hymn 110. "My God, I love thee."

O God, Eternal Father,
We praise and adore thee for thine amazing love;
For the remission of our sins, and the new birth which thou hast given us
In our Saviour Jesus Christ.
Quicken us, we beseech thee, with thy Holy Spirit,

That the bread we break may be unto us
   The body of thy Son, Jesus Christ,
   Who is the True Bread from Heaven,
And the wine his Blood who is the True Vine;
Grant us so to eat his Flesh and drink his Blood
   That he may be in us
   Our strength and gladness,
The Hope of our gory, our light and joy for evermore. Amen.

   Now the God of Peace,
Who brought again from the dead, by the blood of the eternal covenant,
The Great Shepherd of the Sheep, even our Lord Jesus,
   Make us perfect
In every good thing to do his will,
   Working in us
That which is well pleasing in his sight,
Through Jesus Christ; to whom be glory
   For ever and ever. Amen.[*]

18. Our desires — Largely in the nature of meditation.

[*This service is more in the nature of a meditation. The prayers want saying slowly, and the hymn can be sung quite quietly kneeling.*]

God limits his work in the world within the ambit of man's desires. All good has come into life through someone's wanting it. It follows then that man's desires matter to God.

We are in the world as those who seek to know God's will, and to share in the task of creation. If that is so, then in our desires we provide a field through which God can operate.

Let us bring before God all the personal desires of our hearts, acknowledging them openly to ourselves:—
Desires for our own individual life and growth,
> desires for our work in the world;
> desires for this place;
> desires which take a form of which we are ashamed.

Let us pray God to discipline, strengthen and enlarge our desires.

Almighty God, unto whom all hearts be open, all desires known,
> And from whom no secrets are hid;
Cleanse the thoughts of our hearts by the inspiration of thy Holy Spirit,
> That we may perfectly love thee,
> And worthily magnify thy holy name;
>> Through Christ our Lord. Amen.

I am come that they might have life, and that they might have it more abundantly.

This is life eternal, to know thee.

In the vision and knowledge of God is the keystone of true desire.

Let us therefore ardently desire that knowledge for one another, for this parish,* for the children of the parish, for all whom we love.

Almighty God, who doest give us grace with one accord to make our supplications unto thee,

And dost promise that when two or three are gathered together in thy name thou will grant their requests:

Fulfil now, O Lord, the desires and petitions of thy servants as may be most expedient for them,

Granting us in this world knowledge of thy truth

And in the world to come life everlasting. Amen.

Let us confidently desire that for which we were made, and for which the whole creation is waiting, the Revealing of the sons of God.

> Our Father,
> Which art in heaven,
> Hallowed be thy name.
> Thy kingdom come,
> Thy will be done
> On earth, as it is in heaven.
> Give us this day our daily bread,
> And forgive us our trespasses
> As we forgive them that trespass against us,
> And lead us not into temptation,

But deliver us from evil;
For thine is the kingdom, the power and
the glory,
For ever and ever. Amen.

Let us bring to God our desire for Jesus Christ.

V. With thee is the well of life;
R. And in thy light shall we see light.

Hymn 256. "O thou who camest from above."

Everyone that asketh, receiveth;
And he that seeketh, findeth;
And to him that knocketh,
    It shall be opened.

19. The glory that is man's.

[The words of an ancient psalmist.]

O thou Eternal One, our Lord,
What majesty is thine o'er all the world!
Let me sing of this, thy heavenly strength,
Like tiny children lisping out thy praise.

As I look up to the heavens thy fingers made,
The moon and stars that thou hast shaped,
I ask, And what is man, that thou should'st think of him,
What is mortal man that thou should'st heed him?

Yet thou hast made him little less than divine,
Thou hast crowned him with majesty and honour,
Giving him sway o'er all thy hands have made,
With all things underneath his feet.

O thou Eternal One, our Lord,
What majesty is thine o'er all the world!

[The words of a modern philosopher.]

The filaments which unite the finite spirit to its creative source are never severed. God the Creator remains the sustaining element, continually offering himself to the soul he has awakened.
We are become partakers of Christ.

Let us praise God for the glory that is ours through our creation.
And God said, let us make man in our image, after our likeness. And God created man in his own image,

in the image of God created he him.

> V. We bless thee for our creation;
> R. Holy, holy, holy, Lord God of Hosts;
> V. Heaven and earth are full of thy glory;
> R. Glory be to thee, O Lord Most High.

Let us praise God for the glory that is ours in Christ.
In the beginning was the Word,
And the Word was with God,
And the Word was God.
And the Word became flesh,
And dwelt among us—
And we beheld his glory,
Glory as of the only begotten from the Father,
Full of grace and truth.

> V. We bless thee for thine inestimable love
> R. In the redemption of the world by our Lord Jesus Christ.
> V. Thou art the king of Glory, O Christ;
> R. Thou art the everlasting Son of the Father.
> V. Thou that takest away the sins of the world,
> R. Receive our prayer.
> V. Thou that sittest at the right hand of God the Father,
> R. Have mercy upon us.

Let us praise God for the glory that is ours in the Holy Spirit.
All of us with face unveiled,
Gazing on the mirrored glory of our Lord,
Are hourly being transformed into the same likeness,
From a mere reflected glory
Into an inherent glory;
As may well be, since it proceeds

From the Lord, the Spirit.

V. The holy Church throughout all the world
R. Doth acknowledge thee, the Holy Ghost, the Comforter.
V. Hereby know we that we abide in him and he in us
R. Because he hath given us of his Spirit.
V. Now the Lord is the Spirit.
R. Where the Spirit of the Lord is, there is liberty.

LET US PRAY

Glory to thee, Father of us prodigal sons, that even while we are in the far country we know beyond all doubt that we may arise and go to our Father. We thank thee that thy heart of love forgives, even while our own yet condemns. Reassure us with thy pardon and fashion us anew in thine image. Kindle in us a lively sense of our birthright, and stablish us with thy free spirit. Enable us by thy grace to face life as those to whom is given the right and the power to live as sons of God, in one great family, in Christ our Lord. Amen.

HYMN 644. "Songs of praise the angels sang."

The sense that God is so great in goodness, and we so great in glory, as to be his sons, and so rich as to live in communion with him, so united to him that he is in us, and we in him, will make us do all our duties not only with incomparable joy but courage also. It will fill us with zeal and fidelity, and make us to
                Overflow with praises.

20. Our faith.

This is the victory that overcometh the world, even our faith.

Who is he that overcometh, but he that believeth that Jesus is the Son of God?

Which means:—
 Faith in the reality of God;
 Faith in the ultimate triumph of his purpose;
 Faith that even now God reigns in the kingdoms of men;
 Faith in his way of accomplishment;
 Faith in our own vocation to share his triumph.

Shall it be said of us and of our generation, He could there do no mighty work because of their unbelief?

O thou who hast called us to know in ourselves the power of the Resurrection of thy Son Jesus Christ, through fellowship with his sufferings, we confess to thee the sterility of our faith, the fitfulness of our trust, the joylessness of our living; our fear to see too much of thy purpose, lest it call us from the worship of ourselves. We have sinned in our lack of faith in one another, whereby we have hindered the working of thy Spirit in each other; we have refused to understand the way of Incarnation, whereby we have separated ourselves from our fellows, and hindered our approach to thee. Yet, Lord, in our inmost hearts we believe; help thou our unbelief. Increase our faith, that we may go forward into life in the power of thy Son, Jesus Christ our Lord. Amen.

And he laid his right hand upon me, saying,

Fear not; I am the first and the last and the living one; and I was dead; and behold, I am alive for evermore.

Be of good cheer, I have overcome the world.

[All stand]

They sing the song of Moses the servant of God, and the song of the Lamb, saying,

[All together, said antiphonally, or sung to a Psalm chant]

Great and marvellous are thy works,
O Lord God, the Almighty;
Righteous and true are thy ways,
Thou King of the ages.
Who shall not fear, O Lord, and glorify thy name?
For thou art holy.
For all nations shall come and worship before thee,
For thy righteous acts have been made manifest.
   Gloria.

For all thy saints who have died in faith not having received the promises but having seen them and greeted them from afar,

V.   We praise thee, O God.
R.   We give glory unto thee.

For all who have chosen to be evil intreated, counting the reproach of Christ greater riches than any earthly treasure,

V.&R.   We praise thee, *etc.*

For those who have endured as seeing him who is invisible,

V.&R.   We praise thee, *etc.*

For those who from weakness were made strong,

V.&R. We praise thee, *etc.*

For those of whom thou art not ashamed to be called their God,

V.&R. We praise thee, *etc.*

Above all for our Incarnate and Ascended Lord Christ, who is himself the Way, the Truth, and the Life,

V. We praise thee, O God.
R. We give glory unto thee.

Let us commemorate the saints of Britain.

God whom all the saints adore assembled in thy glorious presence from all times and places of thy dominion; who hast gathered us far dwellers of the islands of the sea into the Kingdom of thy Son; and hast adorned our country with many splendid lamps of holiness; grant us worthily to celebrate the saints of Britain by following their footsteps throughout the world whithersoever thou shalt send us, each in his office lowly serving, till all nations confess thy name and all mankind know and fulfil his destiny in Christ; to whom with thee and the Holy Ghost be all honour and glory, world without end. Amen.

And now in humility and faith let us take up the Christian's equipment.*

Here, O Christ, we stand before thee, thy pledged soldiers and servants. Put on us for the work that lies before us the whole armour of God.

Gird thou our loins with truth that we be not ensnared by any shams or self-deception.

Give us a deep hunger after righteousness as our sure breastplate.

Endue our feet with the swiftness of the message of thy peace.

In our left hand be the shield of trust in thee;

In our right our only weapon, thy unfailing word.

Be thou ever over us our eternal salvation, that we may go forth fearing nothing, but everywhere with boldness may make known the mystery of thy glorious gospel whereof thou hast made us thine ambassadors. Amen.

> Hymn 491. "Fight the good fight."

> We are more than conquerors
> Through Him that loved us.

Epilogue.

It was in the early days of the Church. John the Evangelist made a supper and bade to it a group of preachers, teachers and speakers. This, of course, was most exciting, and they went, very thrilled, and thinking what a glorious opportunity it was, and how they should have a chance of asking ever so many things and finding out about ever so many others. And then it did not turnout at all as they had expected. When supper was over John asked, would they like to go and look at the vine outside? What could they do? To have said, "Oh, no, thanks, we'd rather stay here and talk," would not have been manners. So they murmured "Yes," they would like it, and got up to go out, looking down their noses and feeling rather foolish and annoyed. Surely they knew all about his vine; had they not often read about it in his gospel? As they were going out the Easter moon swung up the sky, and one of them said to John, "There's the Easter moon. Isn't it a little early as yet to look at the vine? There won't be anything much to see, the grapes won't even be formed."

"Curious you should say that," John replied, "for that was just what I thought when the Master halted us before it on the night of the Cross. In fact, the vine was a part of his cross."

How could that be? they all queried, for by now they were out, looking at the vine in the moonlight, and its stem was feeble enough stuff to look at, with no form or comeliness of its own that men should want to make anything out of it, not even a cross. And they pointed this out to John.

"Oh, I didn't mean it quite that way," said John. "No,

I know the wood isn't any use as wood, not good enough even to whittle a peg out of, as my friend Ezekiel says. It was rather like this." He made a motion with his hand and they all sat down on the ground in a group round him.

"There was the Master, younger than most of us, going to his death, cut off before he had seen any fruit of his life and love and teaching. What had he got? Just the poor handful that was us, and we, we were like those branches," and he pointed up at the vine. "Not a bit of fruit on us. Here and there a small shoot of greenery with its funny little blossoms, maybe, but no grapes. That was why I said it was part of his cross. And that was what lay behind his appeal that his joy might be in us. The joy of the vine is to have grapes. Look at that stem, all bent on one end only, to pass into the branches its own life. So it has been with him. He had given himself up utterly to us. And he begged us to bear much fruit to the glory of his Father."

While John was speaking they looked at the vine and began to see it with a new significance. The moon lit up the scars left by drastic pruning. There was here and there the place where a branch had been cut right out. And as they looked they feared, and shuddering passed through them. Then John spoke again.

"I know how you feel," he said. "We felt like that too, but the Master told us not to fear. There would be pruning, heavy pruning even, but we should not be utterly cast away, because he had given us his Word of life, and that, flowing from him into us, would make and ever keep us clean. That is what I meant too, when I wrote that his blood cleanses us from all sin. I meant his abounding, abiding life, always passing onwards through us. The blood is in the life."

"Do you know what it means to bear grapes?" said

John. "It means that you, the branch, become as the vine. As the vine gives itself up wholly to put its life into you, so you in like manner give yourself up to pass on that life which is *his* life and has come into you. You pour it into the fruit, and then at last when that is ripe, the hungry hands of men reach out and press it to their thirsting souls, and you are left naked and bare and exhausted. And the whole process has to begin again."

The moon was waning while he spoke, and through the dusk at the other end of the garden came a curious procession, people of all types and colours and sizes. It was headed by a quaint little man between two tall Roman soldiers bearing torches. But though the little man was between them, and his hands tied behind his back, his eager chin and hooked nose stuck out before the soldiers, and his piercing eyes glowed like coals in the darkness. And although he had no music in his voice he led the procession singing lustily the Song of the Road:—

> As unknown, yet well-known;
> As dying and behold we live;
> As poor, yet making many rich;
> As having nothing yet possessing all
> things.

And all the procession joined in the song though in many tongues, in many tunes and keys. There was also one other thing in common about them. They all wore dark violet.

"That will be your garb," said John. "You have properly no colour of your own. Yet both for yourselves and for others you take into yourselves the red of prayer, the blue of healing. You will pray for others, and through prayer draw fresh life into your souls. You will heal the souls of others, and you will desperately need healing. And your friends if they love you will bring to you these gifts of theirs, their prayer and healing love."

So John brought them back to themselves again. Gone was the garden, the procession, the vine, and John. The group looked at one another. Before them on the ground lay a piece of paper. On it was this:—

"That which was from the beginning, that which we have heard, that which we have seen with our own eyes, that which we beheld and our hands handled, concerning the Word of life — and the life was manifested, and we have seen and bear witness and declare the life, the Eternal life, which was with the Father and was manifested unto us — that which we have seen and heard declare we." Underneath were the words, "Your task and your message," and the signature "John," and the picture of a small bunch of grapes.

Appendix. Notes for the drawing up of similar services.

The character of these services is devotional and their chief concern is with God. All concentration on ourselves is a hindrance.

IN FORM, the service should be built on some one idea which should be in close relation to our life. This is the essential idea underlying "family" prayers. It can have a definite bearing on the day's events or interests; if used by a study group it can be a meditation on some passage studied, a thanksgiving for the working out of God's purpose through history, or the consideration from the devotional angle of a subject discussed from the critical angle. Or it may be connected with some current event, Saint's Day, Church festival, or happening in the home. And it must be viewed not merely from the leader's angle, but from the point of view of all taking part.

A DEFINITE STRUCTURE is essential. There must be a clear line of development, close co-ordination and inter-relation between each section. It is not enough to choose a few prayers and a hymn and passage of Scripture in which the subject is mentioned. There must be a connection which leads on from one aspect of the subject to another, e.g. a service begun in a mood of penitence for our share of the world's evil, must contain a resolution to right the wrong so far as in us lies.

IN PRESENTATION, the subject must be looked at from the divine as well as from the human aspect, e.g. if we express penitence for our share in the world's corporate evil, let us also strengthen our resolve to lessen it by dwelling on God's ultimate triumph, Christ's victory over sin and death, or the Holy Spirit's every-present work within creation. Nothing nourishes the life of the spirit more than such dwelling in thought on God and his activity. It is far more valuable for spiritual growth than much penitence or petition.

SILENCE plays a vital part in these services. There should be a large element (1) at the outset before the service begins, so that in the stillness each may be released from surface distractions and make individual preparation for worship; (2) at various intervals, to ensure that each is fully sharing in and carried along by the line of thought, (3) at the close.

COMPOSITION. At the OUTSET, to ensure that everyone quickly grasps the idea, it should be clearly set out. It can then be given out as a title, but should then be followed immediately by an opening sentence or short passage. Sometimes this does instead of a title. The object underlying such opening verses is not, however, merely to emphasise the central idea, but the far more important one of evoking the spirit of wonder which is the basic element in worship.

As to PRAYERS used, they should be varied, as few as possible, simple in language yet with that quality of richness which marks our English Bible. Praise and thanksgiving must never be omitted. They are tonic to the soul. In making up a prayer, eliminate every word which is not essential. An introductory sentence often makes it possible to use a far wider range of prayers than merely those which make direct mention of the subject.

Prayers can often be adapted by alteration, omission or addition. This must be done warily so as not to destroy the existing rhythm and balance. Important in dealing with a familiar prayer, it is vital in handling a collect.

The end of a prayer should be clearly indicated if folk are to respond "Amen." Use "for Christ's sake", "for thy name's sake" and similar phrases, in careful relation to the Person of the Trinity to whom the prayer is addressed.

If using a litany, versicle and response are far easier at the end of the petition than response only. Unless people have a book they are never sure when to come in with "We beseech thee to hear us," so they have to listen to the reading rather than being free to offer the petition; afraid to make a mistake, they are hesitant to come in, and the swing which should characterise a litany is lost. Further, the reader has to read the petition all in one breath for fear that they will come in too soon. All of which detracts from the atmosphere of worship. But if at the end of each petition or set of petitions the reader says, e.g. "Lord, hear our prayer," then people know when to come in with "And let our cry come to thee." Also such a versicle and response gathers up the petitions into a whole, which is dramatically valuable. The best way to tell people the words of response is to say: — (e.g.) "To the words, O thou that hearest prayer, the response is, Unto thee shall all flesh come." You can then repeat the words of the response if you think people need it.

THE CONCLUSION of the service should be either a benediction or ascription, not only to mark clearly the end, but in order to leave the Godward aspect strongly implanted by affirmation. Where the service ends with a hymn, people can kneel again for a moment's silence.

As to the reader himself, he prepares for the service: —

1. by an intellectually careful choice of material. It should all be neatly written out so that there is no difficulty in reading;
2. by using the material devotionally himself beforehand;
3. by a careful arrangement of every detail in advance, e.g. seeing the pianist or organist about the hymn and the particular tune which is familiar, by having every place found in his books and arranged in the place where he is to take prayers, number of hymn ready, etc., so that there is no fumbling, nor hasty turning over the pages. The leader should always get to the place of prayer in advance and make his own final preparation there.

Many people when they begin to lead the worship of others are troubled by shyness, self-consciousness, a sense of strangeness, the need to attend to what they are doing, so that they do not find themselves free to pray. There is only one cure. It lies in the few minutes of silence before worship begins. Dwell not on the fact of leadership, but on the privilege and joy of offering God worship. Lift up your heart to Him. Remember that He is present always and in every place, therefore here and now; indeed the one thing we cannot do is to remove ourselves from His presence. Realise that He accepts with joy this that you do for Him, and His peace will come to flood your soul and drive out all base thoughts and fears. Having used the prayers beforehand yourself devotionally, you will gradually discover that you are not so much reading prayers to the rest as praying in and with them.

POSITION IN WORSHIP should be allowed to play its part. Even when "prayers" have to be in a hall it makes all the difference to kneel for prayer. And now that 6d. rubber kneelers can be had at Woolworth's, kneeling is possible in any place, and the standing to sing gains by contrast. For a small company a circle is as good an arrangement as any. It is quite possible to learn to kneel for prayer with nothing to kneel at. Servers do. We have not yet begun to understand the part of the body in worship. A controlled, reverent position of body is a vast help, because it is sacramental of our worship; it helps to create the spirit that it symbolises. Equally, at the beginning, when we arrive at the place of worship, it is well to take up a position in which we can stay, because if we fidget, it disturbs both ourselves and others.

And let beauty find some place in the setting. Flowers in spring and summer, autumn leaves and berries which last through the winter, a beautiful picture or piece of colour all help, not only by what they are in themselves but because they speak loudly of a desire to make our worship as worthy as may be of our Lord.

Acknowledgements.

To the Rev. G. C. Binyon and his publishers, Messrs. Longmans, Green & Co., for the prayer "Almighty God our heavenly Father," in Service 8, and the prayer after the hymn in Service 17.

To the Right Rev. the Lord Bishop of Coventry for the prayer "O Thou who art heroic love," in Service 4.

To Messrs. Dobells for the quotation from "Traherne" in Service 19.

To the Rev. Canon A. Nairne, D. D., for the prayer "God whom all the saints adore," in Service 20.

To the Oxford University Press and the Authors for the poem by A. Bunston in Service 12, by R. A. Taylor in Service 13, by E. Underhill in Service 13, and the quotation in Service 12 by F. G. Bowles.

To Mr H. Pink for the prayer "Jesus, Master Carpenter," in Service 3.

To the Student Christian Movement for the thanksgiving "Glory to thee" in Service 7; for parts of the litany in Service 10; and of the thanksgiving "God the Father" in Service 10.

In quotations from the Bible I have used the Authorised, Revised and Moffatt's versions, the Prayer-book version of the Psalms, and Way's "Epistles of St. Paul." Besides collects from the Book of Common Prayer, I have used the following:—

In Service 4, a prayer "O God Who fulfillest thy purpose," by Bishop Westcott.

In Service 7, the ascription from "Acts of Devotion."

In Service 9, a prayer from the Liturgy of St. Dionysius, "O God, Father and Origin of Divinity."

In Service 9, a prayer from the 1928 Proposed Book of Common Prayer, "O God who before the Passion."

In Service 9, a prayer from the Gelasian Sacramentary, "O God of unchangeable power."

In Service 15, a collect from "The Splendour of God."

In Service 17, the prayer "Blessed be thy name," by Bishop Ken.

The hymn quoted in Service 1 is by H. Twells.

The quotation at the end of Service 11 is from Goguel, that in Service 19 from Pringle Pattison.

Hymns.

Service No.	Songs of Praise.	English Hymnal.	Ancient and Modern.
1	187	162	160
2	625	471	172
4	300	548	735
5	556	427	548
6	79	15	642
7	632	476	202
8	178	153	157
8	211	178	431
9	249	489	215
10	202	641	437
11	666	499	634*
12	573	437	520
13	180	155	—
15	458	—	671
16	468	375	—
17	110	80	106
18	256	343	698
19	644	481	297
20	491	389	540

Holy, Holy, Holy!

Holy, holy, holy! Lord God Almighty!
Early in the morning our song shall rise to thee.
Holy, holy, holy! Merciful and mighty,
God in three Persons, blessèd Trinity.

Holy, holy, holy! All saints adore thee,
Casting down their golden crowns around the glassy sea;
Cherubim and seraphim falling down before thee,

Which wert, and art, and evermore shalt be.

Holy, holy, holy! Though the darkness hide thee,
Though the sinful human eye thy glory may not see,
Only thou art holy; there is none beside thee,
Perfect in power, in love, and purity.

Holy, holy, holy! Lord God Almighty!
All thy works shall praise thy Name, in earth, and sky, and sea;
Holy, holy, holy! Merciful and mighty,
God in three Persons, blessèd Trinity.

WORDS: Reginald Heber (1783–1826), 1827

Praise to the Holiest in the height

Praise to the Holiest in the height,
And in the depth be praise;
In all His words most wonderful,
Most sure in all His ways.

O loving wisdom of our God!
When all was sin and shame,
A second Adam to the fight
And to the rescue came.

O wisest love! that flesh and blood,
Which did in Adam fail,

Should strive afresh against the foe,
Should strive and should prevail.

And that a higher gift than grace
Should flesh and blood refine,
God's Presence and His very Self,
And Essence all divine.

O generous love! that He, who smote,
In Man for man the foe,
The double agony in Man
For man should undergo.

And in the garden secretly,
And on the Cross on high,
Should teach His brethren, and inspire
To suffer and to die.

Praise to the Holiest in the height,
And in the depth be praise;
In all His words most wonderful,
Most sure in all His ways.

Words: John H. Newman (1801-1890), 1866

God is working his purpose out

God is working his purpose out
As year succeeds to year:
God is working his purpose out,
And the time is drawing near;
Nearer and nearer draws the time,
The time that shall surely be,

When the earth shall be filled
With the glory of God
As the waters cover the sea.

From utmost east to utmost west,
Wherever foot hath trod,
By the mouth of many messengers
Goes forth the voice of God;
Give ear to me, ye continents,
Ye isles, give ear to me,
That earth may filled
With the glory of God
As the waters cover the sea.

What can we do to work God's work,
To prosper and increase
The brotherhood of all mankind--
The reign of the Prince of Peace?
What can we do to hasten the time--
The time that shall surely be,
When the earth shall be filled
With the glory of God
As the waters cover the sea.

March we forth in the strength of God,
With the banner of Christ unfurled,
That the light of the glorious gospel of truth
May shine throughout the world:
Fight we the fight with sorrow and sin
To set their captives free,
That earth may filled
With the glory of God
As the waters cover the sea.

All we can do is nothing worth
Unless God blessed the deed;
Vainly we hope for the harvest-tide
Till God gives life to the seed;
Yet nearer and nearer draws the time,
The time that shall surely be,
When the earth shall be filled
With the glory of God
As the waters cover the sea.

Words: Arthur Campbell Aigner (1841-1919), 1894

Let all the world in every corner sing

Let all the world in every corner sing, my God and King!
The heavens are not too high, His praise may thither fly,
The earth is not too low, His praises there may grow.
Let all the world in every corner sing, my God and King!

Let all the world in every corner sing, my God and King!
The church with psalms must shout, no door can keep them out;
But, above all, the heart must bear the longest part.
Let all the world in every corner sing, my God and King!

Words: George Herbert (1593–1633), 1633

O little town of Bethlehem

O little town of Bethlehem,
How still we see thee lie!
Above thy deep and dreamless sleep
The silent stars go by;
Yet in thy dark streets shineth
The everlasting Light;
The hopes and fears of all the years
Are met in thee tonight.

For Christ is born of Mary;
And gathered all above,
While mortals sleep, the angels keep
Their watch of wondering love.
O morning stars, together
Proclaim the holy birth!
And praises sing to God the King,
And peace to men on earth.

How silently, how silently,
The wondrous gift is given!
So God imparts to human hearts
The blessings of his heaven.
No ear may hear his coming,
But in this world of sin,
Where meek souls will receive him,
Still the dear Christ enters in.

Where children pure and happy
Pray to the blessed Child,
Where misery cries out to thee,
Son of the Mother mild;
Where charity stands watching
And faith holds wide the door,

The dark night wakes, the glory breaks,
And Christmas comes once more.

O holy Child of Bethlehem,
Descend to us, we pray;
Cast out our sin and enter in,
Be born in us today.
We hear the Christmas angels
The great glad tidings tell;
O come to us, abide with us,
Our Lord Emmanuel!

Words: Phillips Brooks (1835-1893), 1867

Rejoice the Lord is King

Rejoice the Lord is King!
Your Lord and King adore!
Rejoice, give thanks and sing,
And triumph evermore.
Lift up your heart!
Lift up your voice!
Rejoice! again I say, rejoice!

Jesus, the Savior reigns,
The God of truth and love:
When he had purged our stains,
He took his seat above.
Lift up your heart!
Lift up your voice!
Rejoice! again I say, rejoice!

His kingdom cannot fail;

He rules o'er earth and heaven;
The keys of death and hell
Are to our Jesus given.
Lift up your heart!
Lift up your voice!
Rejoice! again I say, rejoice!

He sits at God's right hand
Till all his foes submit,
And bow to his command,
And fall beneath his feet:
Lift up your heart!
Lift up your voice!
Rejoice! again I say, rejoice!

Rejoice in glorious hope!
Jesus the Judge shall come
And take his servants up
To their eternal home:
We soon shall hear the archangel's voice,
The trump of God shall sound: rejoice!

Words: Charles Wesley (1707-1788), 1744

Disposer supreme

Disposer supreme, and Judge of the earth,
who choosest for thine the weak and the poor;
to frail earthen vessels, and things of no worth,
entrusting thy riches which ay shall

endure.

Those vessels soon fail, though full of thy light,
and at thy decree are broken and gone;
thence brightly appeareth the arm of thy might,
as through the clouds breaking the lightnings have shone.

Like clouds are they borne to do thy great will,
and swift as the winds about the world go:
the Word with his wisdom their spirits doth fill;
they thunder, they lighten, the waters o'erflow.

Their sound goeth forth, "Christ Jesus is Lord!"
Then Satan doth fear, his citadels fall;
as when the dread trumpets went forth at thy word,
and on the ground lieth the Canaanite's wall.

O loud be their trump, and stirring their sound,
to rouse us, O Lord, from sin's deadly sleep.
May lights which thou kindlest in darkness around
the dull soul awaken her vigils to keep!

All honor and praise, dominion and might,
to God, Three in One, eternally be,
who round us hath shed his own marvelous light,
and called us from darkness his glory to see.

Words: Jean-Baptiste de Santeüil (1630-1697), 1686
Translation: Isaac Williams (1802–1865), 1836

The Church's one foundation

The Church's one foundation
Is Jesus Christ her Lord;
She is his new creation,
By water and the word:
From heaven he came and sought her
To be his holy bride;
With his own blood he bought her,
And for her life he died.

Elect from every nation,
Yet one o'er all the earth,
Her charter of salvation,
One Lord, one faith, one birth;
One holy Name she blesses,
Partakes one holy food,
And to one hope she presses,
With every grace endued.

Though with a scornful wonder
Men see her sore oppressed,

By schisms rent asunder,
By heresies distressed;
Yet saints their watch are keeping,
Their cry goes up, "How long?"
And soon the night of weeping
Shall be the morn of song.

Mid toil and tribulation,
And tumult of her war
She waits the consummation
Of peace for evermore;
Till with the vision glorious
Her longing eyes are blessed,
And the great Church victorious
Shall be the Church at rest.

Yet she on earth hath union
With God, the Three in one,
And mystic sweet communion
With those whose rest is won.
O happy ones and holy!
Lord, give us grace that we
Like them, the meek and lowly,
On high may dwell with thee.

Words: Samuel John Stone (1839-1900), 1866

For all the saints

For all the saints, who from their labors rest,
Who thee by faith before the world

confessed,
Thy Name, O Jesus, be forever blessed.
Alleluia, Alleluia!

Thou wast their Rock, their Fortress and their Might;
Thou, Lord, their Captain in the well fought fight;
Thou, in the darkness drear, their one true Light.
Alleluia, Alleluia!

For the apostles' glorious company,
Who bearing forth the cross o'er land and sea,
Shook all the mighty world, we sing to Thee:
Alleluia, Alleluia!

For the Evangelists, by whose blest word,
Like fourfold streams, the garden of the Lord,
Is fair and fruitful, be thy Name adored.
Alleluia, Alleluia!

For Martyrs, who with rapture kindled eye,
Saw the bright crown descending from the sky,
And seeing, grasped it, thee we glorify.
Alleluia, Alleluia!

O may thy soldiers, faithful, true, and bold,
Fight as the saints who nobly fought of

old,
And win, with them the victor's crown of gold.
Alleluia, Alleluia!

O blest communion, fellowship divine!
We feebly struggle, they in glory shine;
All are one in thee, for all are thine.
Alleluia, Alleluia!

And when the strife is fierce, the warfare long,
Steals on the ear the distant triumph song,
And hearts are brave, again, and arms are strong.
Alleluia, Alleluia!

The golden evening brightens in the west;
Soon, soon to faithful warriors comes their rest;
Sweet is the calm of paradise the blessed.
Alleluia, Alleluia!

But lo! there breaks a yet more glorious day;
The saints triumphant rise in bright array;
The King of glory passes on his way.
Alleluia, Alleluia!

From earth's wide bounds, from ocean's farthest coast,
Through gates of pearl streams in the countless host,

And singing to Father, Son and Holy Ghost:
Alleluia, Alleluia!

Words: William Walsham How (1823-1897), 1864

There's a wideness in God's mercy

There's a wideness in God's mercy
like the wideness of the sea;
there's a kindness in his justice,
which is more than liberty.
There is welcome for the sinner,
and more graces for the good;
there is mercy with the Savior;
there is healing in his blood.

There is no place where earth's sorrows
are more felt than in heaven;
there is no place where earth's failings
have such kind judgment given.
There is plentiful redemption
in the blood that has been shed;
there is joy for all the members
in the sorrows of the Head.

For the love of God is broader
than the measure of man's mind;
and the heart of the Eternal
is most wonderfully kind.
If our love were but more faithful,
we should take him at his word;

and our life would be thanksgiving
for the goodness of the Lord.

Words: Frederick William Faber (1814-1863), 1862

Love divine

Love divine, all loves excelling,
Joy of heaven to earth come down;
Fix in us thy humble dwelling;
All thy faithful mercies crown!
Jesus, Thou art all compassion,
Pure unbounded love Thou art;
Visit us with Thy salvation;
Enter every trembling heart.

Breathe, O breathe Thy loving Spirit,
Into every troubled breast!
Let us all in Thee inherit;
Let us find that second rest.
Take away our bent to sinning;
Alpha and Omega be;
End of faith, as its Beginning,
Set our hearts at liberty.

Come, Almighty to deliver,
Let us all Thy life receive;
Suddenly return and never,
Never more Thy temples leave.
Thee we would be always blessing,
Serve Thee as Thy hosts above,
Pray and praise Thee without ceasing,

Glory in Thy perfect love.

Finish, then, Thy new creation;
Pure and spotless let us be.
Let us see Thy great salvation
Perfectly restored in Thee;
Changed from glory into glory,
Till in heaven we take our place,
Till we cast our crowns before Thee,
Lost in wonder, love, and praise.

Words: Charles Wesley (1707-1788), 1747

Come, thou holy Paraclete

Come, Thou holy Paraclete,
And from Thy celestial seat
Send Thy light and brilliancy:
Father of the poor, draw near;
Giver of all gifts, be here;
Come, the soul's true radiancy.

Come, of comforters the best,
Of the soul the sweetest guest,
Come in toil refreshingly:
Thou in labor rest most sweet,
Thou art shadow from the heat,
Comfort in adversity.

O Thou Light, most pure and blest,
Shine within the inmost breast
Of Thy faithful company.

Where Thou art not, man hath naught;
Every holy deed and thought
Comes from Thy divinity.

What is soilèd, make Thou pure;
What is wounded, work its cure;
What is parchèd, fructify;
What is rigid, gently bend;
What is frozen, warmly tend;
Strengthen what goes erringly.

Fill Thy faithful, who confide
In Thy power to guard and guide,
With Thy sevenfold mystery.
Here Thy grace and virtue send:
Grant salvation to the end,
And in Heav'n felicity.

Words: Unknown author, 12th Century (*Veni Sancte Spiritus*)
Translation: John Mason Neale (1818-1866), 1854

Breathe on me, breath of God

Breathe on me, breath of God,
Fill me with life anew,
That I may love what Thou dost love,
And do what Thou wouldst do.

Breathe on me, breath of God,
Until my heart is pure,
Until with Thee I will one will,

To do and to endure.

Breathe on me, breath of God,
Blend all my soul with Thine,
Until this earthly part of me
Glows with Thy fire divine.

Breathe on me, breath of God,
So shall I never die,
But live with Thee the perfect life
Of Thine eternity.

Words: Edwin Hatch (1835-1889), 1878

City of God, how broad and far

City of God, how broad and far
Outspread thy walls sublime!
The true thy chartered freemen are
Of every age and clime.

One holy Church, one army strong;
One steadfast, high intent;
One working band, one harvest song,
One King omnipotent.

How purely hath thy speech come down
From man's primeval youth!
How grandly hath thine empire grown
Of freedom, love and truth!

How gleam thy watch fires through the

night
With never fainting ray!
How rise thy towers, serene and bright,
To meet the dawning day!

In vain the surge's angry shock,
In vain the drifting sands;
Unharmed upon the eternal Rock
The eternal City stands.

Words: Samuel Johnson (1822-1882), 1864

My God, I love thee

My God, I love Thee; not because
I hope for Heav'n thereby,
Nor yet because who love Thee not
May eternally die.

Thou, O my Jesus, Thou didst me
Upon the cross embrace;
For me didst bear the nails and spear,
And manifold disgrace.

And griefs and torments numberless,
And sweat of agony;
E'en death itself; and all for man
Who was Thine enemy.

Then why, O blessèd Jesus Christ
Should I not love Thee well?
Not for the hope of winning Heaven,

Nor of escaping hell.

Not with the hope of gaining aught,
Nor seeking a reward,
But as Thyself hast lovèd me,
O everlasting Lord!

E'en so I love Thee, and will love,
And in Thy praise will sing,
Solely because Thou art my God,
And my eternal King.

Words: Unknown author (*O Deus, ego amo te*)
Translation: Edward Caswall (1814-1878), 1849

O thou who camest from above

O thou who camest from above,
The pure celestial fire to impart
Kindle a flame of sacred love
Upon the mean altar of my heart.

There let it for thy glory burn
With inextinguishable blaze,
And trembling to its source return,
In humble prayer and fervent praise.

Jesus, confirm my heart's desire
To work and speak and think for thee;
Still let me guard the holy fire,
And still stir up thy gift in me.

Ready for all thy perfect will,
My acts of faith and love repeat,
Till death thy endless mercies seal,
And make my sacrifice complete.

Words: Charles Wesley (1707-1788), 1762

Songs of praise the angels sang

Songs of praise the angels sang,
Heaven with alleluias rang,
When creation was begun,
When God spoke and it was done.

Songs of praise awoke the morn
When the Prince of Peace was born;
Songs of praise arose when he
Captive led captivity.

Heaven and earth must pass away;
Songs of praise shall crown that day;
God will make new heavens and earth;
Songs of praise shall hail their birth.

And will man alone be dumb
Till that glorious kingdom come?
No; the Church delights to raise
Psalms and hymns and songs of praise.

Saints below, with heart and voice,
Still in songs of praise rejoice,
Learning here, by faith and love,

Songs of praise to sing above.

Borne upon their latest breath,
Songs of praise shall conquer death;
Then, amidst eternal joy,
Songs of praise their powers employ.

Hymns of glory, songs of praise,
Father, unto thee we raise,
Jesus, glory unto thee,
With the Spirit, ever be.

Words: James Montgomery (1771–1854), 1819

Fight the good fight

Fight the good fight with all thy might;
Christ is thy Strength, and Christ thy Right;
Lay hold on life, and it shall be
Thy joy and crown eternally.

Run the straight race through God's good grace,
Lift up thine eyes, and seek His face;
Life with its way before us lies,
Christ is the Path, and Christ the Prize.

Cast care aside, upon thy Guide,
Lean, and His mercy will provide;
Lean, and the trusting soul shall prove
Christ is its Life, and Christ its Love.

Faint not nor fear, His arms are near,
He changeth not, and thou art dear.
Only believe, and thou shalt see
That Christ is all in all to thee.

WORDS: John Samuel Bewley Monsell (1811-1875), 1863

Notes.

4. The purpose of God.

*. These two petitions arose out of subjects of reading and discussion. For them can be substituted petitions bearing on the immediate subjects of your own reading and interests. Only keep the vision of God wide. You can have as many petitions as you like, and then you would make a regular versicle and response. (V. "We praise thee;" R. "Praying that thy kingdom come," which you would use till the last petition "for light and life and love." (See App., p. 72.)

17. Preparation for Holy Communion.

*. NOTE .— This isn't perhaps, the sort of preparation you are accustomed to use before Communion: especially do you wonder why there is so little about individual self-examination in it. Before rejecting it, at least know the reason, which is twofold. First, that God is infinitely greater than our sins; and to be concerned with his glory and to praise him is our duty; and comes long before the consideration of our miserable misdeeds, as the Lord's prayer itself teaches us. Second, that if we do achieve some realisation, however partial, of the truth and beauty of his love, we shall be strong to forsake our sins, which is more to the point than bewailing them.

18. Our desires.

*. Local references: each leader can supply his own.

20. Our faith.

*. This prayer may well be said, one knee on the ground, the other bent, ready for action, as in old pictures of God's messengers, knights and angels.

Hymns.

*. Slightly different wording.

www.ingramcontent.com/pod-product-compliance
Lightning Source LLC
Chambersburg PA
CBHW071311060426
42444CB00034B/1771